MOST WANTED APPLE RECIPES

YOUR FAVORITE DISHES AT YOUR FINGERTIPS

Table Of Content

Apple and Onion Pie

Ingredients:

6 ounces apples

1 egg (hard boiled)

Butter

1/4 pound of onions (Spanish)

Salt

Pepper

Ready-made pie crust

Instructions:

Peel onion and apples then cut into slices. Place in small cooking pot and stew, adding little amount of water.

Once onions and apples are almost tender, add in butter and enough salt and pepper to taste. Pour over small pie plate.

Slice the eggs into four equal cuts and arrange egg slices on top of mixture and cover w/ crust. Bake for 30 mins.

Apple and Peach Meringue Pie

Ingredients:

Apples

Peaches

Nutmeg

3 eggwhites

3 Tbsps of powdered sugar

Vanilla

Ready-made pie crust

Instructions:

Stew peaches and apples, adding enough sugar as desired to sweeten. Mash 'til smooth, then season w/ nutmeg.

Scoop into pie crust, filling 'til the brim. Bake 'til done.

Meanwhile, whip eggwhites 'til frothy but stiff and add sugar. Add in vanilla to flavor, beating well 'til hard peaks form. Spread 1/2" - 1" thick of meringue into pie. Bake again 'til meringue sets.

Apple Butter with Cider

Ingredients:

Apples; pared, cored and quartered

Cider

Cinnamon powder

Cloves

Nutmeg

Instructions:

Fill one big kettle w/ cider, boil 'til volume is reduced into half. Place enough apples in thee kettle, enough to be moistened by cider, stirring frequently.

When apples turns soft, remove using skimmer w/ holes and transfer to a small tub. Repeat procedure, adding more chopped apples into cider.

Large amount of apple butter requires stewing overnight.

Leave apples on tub, covered w/ clean cloth overnight to completely cool. The following day, boil cider & apple again 'til it creates a marmalade-like consistency and color turns very deep brown.

Apple Butter without Cider

Ingredients:

10 gallons of water

6 gallons of molasses

8 bushels of apple; pared, cored and quartered

1 lb of mixed spice (cloves, allspice, cinnamon and nutmeg); finely powdered

Instructions:

Combine water and molasses in kettle large enough to accommodate these fluids. Boil, then skim so long as scums continue rising.

Reserve one-half of liquid then transfer into tub. Prepare 8 bushels apples and gradually throw into boiling liquid.

Continue hard boiling. Once thickened, gradually add reserved water-molasses mixture, stirring frequently in order to avoid scorching. Make sure it has equal consistencies all throughout.

Continue boiling for 10-12 hrs, continuously stirring. Remove mixture from kettle in the evening and cool in large tubs, covered.

The following morning, have the mixture boiled again for additional 6-8 hrs (total of 18 hrs). Thirty minutes prior to removing, add in mixed spices. Once done, pour into stone jars.

Apple Cake - Version 1

Ingredients:

6 ozs of wheat-meal (Allinson, fine)

4.5 of butter

3 ozs of castor sugar

1 pc of egg

6 ozs of flour (white)

1.5 lbs of apples; sliced thinly

1 tsp of cinnamon

Water (cold)

Instructions:

Rub butter on flour and meal then add beaten egg then as needed in making paste, add water (cold). Roll into 1/4" thick then line flat tin (buttered) with mixture. Stick and arrange apples on mixture, pointing down. Pour the remaining mixture thinly on apples.

Bring edges in bottom and edges in top together, making two incisions then bake over medium-hot oven 'til cake is brown. Allow to be cooled before sifting sugar (Castor) on it. Slice into several pieces.

Apple Cake - Version 2

Ingredients:

1.5 c of flour; sifted

3 tsps of baking powder; sifted

1/2 tsp of salt; sifted

2 Tbsps of shortening

4-5 pcs of apples ; pared and sliced

1/2 c of sugar

1/2 c of milk

1 tsp of cinnamon

Instructions:

Rub shortening into combined and sifted ingredients together. Gradually pour milk into mixture then mix to create dough that is soft. Put mixture on bread board that has been floured then roll into1/2" thick. Place in shallow pan that has been greased.

Press apples to the dough then sprinkle cinnamon and sugar. Bake for half an hour in moderate-hot oven 'til apples become brown and tender. Serve while warm together with cream or milk.

Apple Charlotte - Version 1

Ingredients:

2 lbs apples (for cooking); pared and sliced

2 ozs almonds; chopped

4 ozs sultanas and currants (mixed)

1 stick cinnamon (approximately 3" long)

Lemon juice (from half a lemon)

Bread and butter (Allinson); sliced thinly

Sugar (to taste)

Instructions:

Stew apples together with cinnamon as well as teacupful water 'til apples become pulpy. Take away cinnamon then add sultanas and currants, almonds, juice and sugar. Mix well then let mixture cool.

Line a buttered pie dish with the Allinson slices and top with cooked mixture. Create layers of Allinson and apples mixture, with the Allinson on top as final layer. Bake 45 minutes in medium hot oven.

Apple Charlotte - Version 2

Ingredients:

Apples (juicy); peel and sliced

Sugar (castor)

Rind of lemon; grated

Nutter or butter

Bread crumbs

Instructions:

Butter or oil a pie dish and coat thinly using crumbs. Place several pieces of nutter, topped with apples and sprinkled with rind and sugar. Repeat layers 'til dish becomes full. Put crumbs as last layer on top.

Bake 20-30 minutes. Turn on dish carefully then drizzle sugar (castor) on it. Serve cold or hot partnered with custard (boiled) if preferred.

Apple Cream

Ingredients:

Apples (very ripe); quartered

Doubled refined sugar; sifted

Eggwhites

Instructions:

Scald quarted apples 'til soft. Once done, pare then mash clear apple part. Sieve pulp.

Beat together apples and sugar. Beat separately eggwhites 'til stiff, then add into apple mixture. Scoop into dish at once.

Apple Custard Pie - Version 1

Ingredients:

3 c of milk

4 pcs of eggs

1 c of sugar

2 c of stewed apples (strained through a colander)

Flavoring with nutmeg

Instructions:

Beat egg yolks and egg whites. Place yolks in a mixing bowl, add apples, and flavoring; mix them well.

Add milk then last the egg whites; mix thoroughly. Pour onto a half-baked crust and bake like any custard pie.

Apple Custard Pie - Version 2

Ingredients:

Apples (sour); peeled

3 pcs of eggs (for one pie)

1/3 c of butter (for one pie)

1/3 c of sugar (for one pie)

Nutmeg

Instructions:

Stew the apples till softened and water inside has reduced to almost gone. Rub stewed apples through strainer.

Beat eggs then add sugar and butter. Combine with the apples then season it with ground nutmeg.

Apple Dumplings - Version 1

Ingredients:

Apples

Sugar

Cinnamon

Instructions:

You can use lots of apples when required. Core the apples. Mix cinnamon and sugar; place them on the hollow of the apples. Make paste to make small crust, then roll out. Wrap the apples with the crust.

Bake dumplings inside oven for 30-40 mins or let them boil in water, place dumplings inside the boiling water if it is boiling fast. You can serve dumplings with any white (sweet) sauce or whip cream.

Apple Dumplings - Version 2

Ingredients:

6 pcs of Codlins (or any good apples)

Butter paste

Water

Salt

Instructions:

Pare then core the apples. Make small amount of cold (butter) paste, roll up as thick as the finger, lap it around on each apple then tie inside a (fine) cloth and boil the apples in water with salt.

Let it boil first before placing the apples inside. Serve with sugar or white (wine) sauce with butter.

Apple Dumplings - Version 3

Ingredients:

Apples

Sugar

Clove

Instructions:

Peel then core the apples. Fill its hollow with clove and sugar. Make paste then cut to squares and wrap each apple with it. Bake for 30-40 mins or boil them by tying them using a fine cloth and place them inside the water only after it has boiled. Cook for 45-60 mins.

Apple Dumplings - Version 4

Ingredients:

Apples

Sugar

Cinnamon

Instructions:

Make a (rich biscuit) dough; pinch off a chunk and roll it out to a thin crust for pie. Cut to squares, enough for the size of apples. Pare and core the apples then slice them in half.

Place two pieces of apples (half) in the crust and sprinkle cinnamon then sugar on them. Wrap the apples tightly.

Arrange dumpling onto a buttered dripping pan, with smoothened side facing up. Place butter atop of every dumpling and sprinkle lots of refined sugar then turn in one cup of (boiling) water.

Bake moderately for 45 mins. Baste once with liquor. Serve dumplings with sugar, cream or pudding-sauce.

Apple Egg Pie

Ingredients:

6 eggs; boiled

6 pcs apples

1 & 1/2 lb of beef-suet

1 lb of currants

Mace

Sugar

Nutmeg

1-2 tsps of brandy

Instructions:

Shred eggs, apples, beef-suet and currants. Season enough nutmeg, mace & sugar as desired to taste. Add in 1-2 tsps brandy as desired.sugar, cream or pudding-sauce.

Apple Filling

Ingredients:

1 c of sugar

1 pc of egg

3 pcs of large apples; grated

1 pc of lemon (juiced and zested)

Instructions:

Combine sugar, egg, apples. lemon zest and juice inside a saucepan; stir together. Cook until thickened. Let it cool before using.

Apple Fool

Ingredients:

4 c of fresh apples

1 c of dates; pitted

1-1/2 c of evaporated milk

1/2 c of cream

6 pcs of cloves (tied in muslin)

Sugar

Instructions:

Pare and core apples, then cut them up. Slowly stew apples, dates, cloves with (teacupful) water till tender. Once cooked, discard cloves.

Rub fruits through mesh strainer and gradually add milk and cream, in which mixture should continue boiling. Serve them cold.

Apple Fritters - Version 1

Ingredients:

4 pcs of eggs (large)

4 Tbsps of flour (fine quality)

1/2 c of refined sugar

Nutmeg, Salt, and Milk (as necessary)

Apples; pared and cored

Instructions:

Beat the eggs then add flour, milk, sugar, salt, and nutmeg. Mix thoroughly, but don't make the mixture thin.

Slice the (pared and cored) apples to rounds. Heat a skillet with oil. Once the oil is very hot, dip apple slices into the batter and fry them till slightly brown. Drain excess oil on paper towel. Serve with sauce: sugar, (white) wine, and butter.

Apple Fritters - Version 2

Ingredients:

1 c of sweet milk

2 c of flour

2 pcs of eggs (beat the yolks and white separately)

1 Tbsp of sugar

1 Tbsp of salt

Apples; pared, cored and sliced thinly

Instructions:

Heat milk then place on a mixing bowl, add sugar, egg yolks then stir thoroughly. Add egg whites and flour; incorporate well.

Dip the apples into batter. Heat skillet with oil, once very hot, place a spoonful of apples; fry till slightly brown.

Drain excess oil with paper towel. Serve at once with syrup (maple or clarified sugar).

Apple Ginger

Ingredients:

4 lbs of apple; chopped finely

4 lbs of sugar

1 pint of water

1 oz of green ginger

Lemon rind (from 4 lemons); grated

Instructions:

Create syrup by combining sugar and water. Pour chopped apples and ginger in and combine grated lemon rind.

Boil in low-heat for 2 hrs or 'til clear in color.

Apple Jelly - Version 1

Ingredients:

2 c of Apples; rinsed and cut

2 c of water

2 c of loaf sugar

2 c of juice (lemon)

Instructions:

Boil (rinsed and cut) apples in water till tender. Pour onto a (jelly) bag then drain. Boil (loaf) sugar and lemon juice, skim carefully, for 2-3 hours.

Apple Jelly - Version 2

Ingredients:

Apples; sliced

Water

2 c of sugar (for every 2 cups of liquid)

Half the juice of 1 lemon (for every 2 cups of liquid)

Instructions:

Place the apple slices inside a (porcelain) kettle then cover water. Cook gently till apples seem red then pour onto colander to drain its juice onto a jelly bag then return liquid onto a clean kettle. Boil for 30 mins.

Measure the liquid, add juice then sugar; let it boil for 10 mins.

Apple Jelly - Version 3

Ingredients:

20 pcs of large ripe apples (pippins); pare, core, chopped

Zests from 4 pcs of yellow lemon; grated

Lemon juice (from the grated 4 lemons)

Water

2 c of sugar loaf (for every 2 c of liquid)

Instructions:

Place apples inside a clean jar. Add lemon zests then cover them tightly. Place jar on a large pot with water. Let water boil until apples dissolve. Strain through the jelly bag then mix liquid with juice.

Measure the combined liquid then add sugar loaf; place inside (porcelain) kettle. When sugar has melted, place kettle above heat and let it boil; skim for every 20 mins until it thickens like a jelly. Place inside tumblers then cover with paper towels and a lid.

Apple Leather

Ingredients:

6 lbs of ripe apples; pared and quartered

3 lbs of brown sugar

Instructions:

Mix together sugar and apples in kettle w/ very little water. Once done, mash and pound using a big wooden spoon. Boil & skim for 3 hrs more, frequently stirring.

Once done, spread into large storage dishes then place under direct sunlight for 3-4 days.

Loosen leathers form dishes then place in hot but turned off oven. Let it remain inside your oven 'til it cools.

Apple Pie - Version 1

Ingredients:

1-1/2 c of flour; sifted

1-1/2 tsps of baking powder (Calumet)

1/2 tsp of salt

1/3 c of shortening

Water (cold)

4 pcs of apples; rinsed, pared, cored and sliced

4 Tbsps of sugar

1 Tbsp of butter (unsalted)

Nutmeg or Cinnamon

Confectioner's sugar; sifted

Instructions:

Combine flour, salt, and Calumet inside a mixing bowl. Add the shortening then rub very gently and add enough amount of water, making the dough firm.

Roll 1/2 of the dough out onto a floured surface. Roll to a thin crust and line a pie dish.

Place apples inside; sprinkle sugar then dot bits of unsalted butter. Sprinkle nutmeg or cinnamon then wet the crust edges with (cold) water. Cover with pastry then seal the edges and trim excess pastry.

Poke holes on top using a fork then bake moderately for half an hour. Dust confectioner's sugar on top then serve while hot or warm.

Apple Pie - Version 2

Ingredients:

2 pcs of cooking apples (medium-sized); pared, cored, and cut up

Sugar

Cinnamon

Lemon zest

Pastry

Instructions:

Place apples inside a pie dish (lined with pastry), sprinkle sugar, cinnamon and small amount of water then cover pastry on top. Bake on high heat till browned then reduce the heat to low and continue to bake for 15 mins.

Apple Pudding - Version 1

Ingredients:

6 pcs of baking apples; cored

2 Tbsps of refined sugar

1-1/2 c of whole milk

3 pcs of eggs

12 Tbsps of wholemeal (Allinson)

1 tsp of cinnamon (ground)

2 Tbsps of melted butter

Instructions:

Mix cinnamon with sugar; place onto the hollows of cored apple. Place apples onto buttered pie dish. Combine eggs, milk, wheatmeal, and butter; pour onto the dish with apples. Bake moderately for two hours.

Apple Pudding - Version 2

Ingredients:

6 pcs of large apple (codlins or pippens)

8 pcs of eggs (large)

1 c of sugar

1 c of clarified butter

Lemon zest

Bread crumbs (or biscuit)

Orange (or citron)

Instructions:

Roast the apples and remove pulp. Get the eggs, but leave out 6 whites, and the sugar then beat them well and place on the apple pulp. Add butter, zest, crumbs, orange. Bake with (thin) paste beneath it.

Apple Roll

Ingredients:

4 apples (medium-sized); peeled, cored and finely chopped

2 c of water

1 & 1/2 c of sugar

Rich biscuit dough

Cinnamon

Plain or whipped cream

Instructions:

Cook water & sugar in bake pan placed over low-fire. Roll 1/2-inch thick of ready-made dough, spread w/ apples, then roll up into long dough roll. Slice into 2-inch long pieces.

Arrange w/ cut-side-down in warmed syrup, top w/ small butter piece then dust w/ sugar & cinnamon.

Bake 'til fruit is done & crust is golden-browned. Place on serving platter, drizzle w/ syrup then top w/ cream.

Apple Shake

Ingredients:

1/2 peeled orange w/ pithy-part unremoved

1 banana (ripe)

1 slice of orange for garnising purposes

1 Tbsp of brewer's yeast

2 apples (greed); seeded

Instructions:

Squeeze out juices from apples and orange. Combine juices, yeast and banana in blender, then well 'til smooth.

Top w/ a thin piece of sliced orange.

Apple Souffle - Version 1

Ingredients:

1 pint of apple; steamed

1 Tbsp butter; melted

1/2 c of sugar

6 eggwhites

3 eggyolks; well beaten

Nutmeg

Instructions:

Add butter, nutmeg, eggyolks and sugar into steamed apples. Blend well. Beat eggwhites 'til frothy and stiff. Once apple mixture cools, blend in eggwhites.

Grease a 3-pint bake dish then turn out souffle into dish. Have it baked for 30 mins in moderate-heat oven.

Apple Souffle - Version 2

Ingredients:

4 pcs eggs

2 ounces sugar (castor)

4 pcs pared apples

1 glass new milk

1 ounce of cornflour (Allinson)

Lemon juice; extracted from 1 lemon

Instructions:

Slice apples then stew w/ sugar & juice 'til reduced into pulps. Beat gently and return into stewpan.

Smoothen cornflour w/ milk, then blend into apples, stirring well 'til mixture boils. Pour into small basin when done to have it cooled completely.

Separate eggyolks and eggwhites. Beat yolks vigorously and blend into apple mix. Whisk eggwhites 'til frothy and stiff and combine into prepared mixture.

Pour batter into greased souffle pan.Bake it for twenty minutes at moderate-heat, then serve when done.

Apple Soup

Ingredients:

1 pc of large apple (cooking); peel then cut up

1 pc of small onion; chopped finely

Sugar and seasoning (to taste)

Butter

1 tsp of flour (corn)

1 c of water.

Instructions:

Cook onion and apple in water until almost tendered. Rub mixture to a mesh strainer and return inside saucepan then add butter, sugar, and seasoning.

Add flour till soup thickens. Serve at once.

Apple Tansey

Ingredients:

Apples; pared

Sweetened butter

10 eggs

Sweet cream

Nutmeg

Cinnamon

Ginger

Sugar

Rose-water

Instructions:

Cut pared apples into thin rounded slices. Place butter and app less in fry pan & fry the apples.

Separately combine, eggs, cream, cinnamon, nutmeg, sugar, rose-water and ginger together. Mix thoroughly then pour into apples, then have them fried.

Apple Tart - Version 1

Ingredients:

2 pounds apples; pared, cored, sliced

2 ounces of almonds; chopped

12 ounces of fine-wheat meal (Allinson)

1 c of sultanas and currants

1 tsp of powdered cinnamon

4 & 1/2 ounces of butter

Water

Sugar

Instructions:

Stew apples w/ little amount of water. When almost done, you add in sultanas, currants, cinnamon, sugar and almonds. Simmer ingredients together 'til apples turns into pulp, then cool apple.

Blend wheat meal w/ water and little amount of butter 'til paste-looking. Roll out & line 1 rounded, flat bake dish w/ the paste. Brush paste w/ eggwhites. Turn apple mix out into paste.

Cut remaining paste into 3/8-inch wide strips. Arrange over apples, creating diamond-shape, one inch apart. If there is enough of paste remaining, lay one thin paste strip around edge of dish. Mark nicely w/ fork.

Bake for 45 mins, then serve w/ custard.

Apple Tarts - Version 2

Ingredients:

1/2 c water

10 large tart apples; pared and quartered

6 eggyolks

Lemon juice from 2 lemons

Lemon peel from 2 lemons

1/2 c of butter

1 & 1/2 - 2 c of sugar

Puff paste

Instructions:

Core & boil apples in 1/2 c water 'til soft, beat 'til smooth. Add in eggyolks, lemon juice, lemon peel, butter and sugar, blending all ingredients thoroughly.

Prepare and line your patty-pans w/ puff-paste and pour mixture in. Bake for 5 mins in well-heated oven.

Apple Trifle

Ingredients:

Tart apples; peeled, cored and quartered

Orange and quince rind

Sugar

1 pint of whipped cream; flavored w/ lemon peel

Instructions:

Stew apples and 1 strip each of your quince and orange rind w/ enough water, covering bottom part of stewpan. Then add in sugar (1/2 lb sugar to 1 lb of fruit).

Once cooked, squeeze the fruit pulp gently through sieve. When pulp cools, pour into a deep dish then top w/ one pint lemon-flavored whipped-cream.

Apple-Grape Salad

Ingredients:

1 Tbsp of gelatin (unflavored)

1/2 c of halved & seeded red grapes

1 /4 c of celery; chopped

1 c of Fuji or Rome apples, unpaired and diced

1/4 c of water

1 & 1/2 c of apple-flavored juice

Instructions:

Combine and gelatin w/ water and soften for five minutes. Place over low-heat, constantly stirring 'til well dissolved. Pour in apple-flavored juice, mix well.

Chill 'til mixture thickened and add in apples, grapes and chopped celery. Place in 3-cup sized mold and chill 'til set.

Baked Apples

Ingredients:

12 apples; pared and cored

Brown sugar

Lemon juice

Lemon rind

Sweetened whipped cream (lemon-flavored)

Instructions:

Arrange apples side-by-side in large-sized bake pan filled w/ small amount of water. Fill cored holes w/ sugar and pour in small amounts of juice. Insert beautifully cut lemon rind into each apple.

Bake apples for 60 mins or 'til tender (avoid breaking apples). Once done, remove from pan and cool completely, placing them on covered containers.

Serve w/ a scoop of flavored whipped cream placed all over your apples.

Boiled Apple Puffets

Ingredients:

3 eggs

1 pint of milk

Flour

Salt

1 & 1/2 tsps of baking powder

Finely chopped apples

Instructions:

Combine eggs, milk, salt, powder and enough flour in order to create a thick waffle-batter. Fill your teacups w/ batter layer, alternate w/ chopped apples.

Steam for 60 minutes. Best when served hot w/ sugar and cream w/ flavor..

Butterscotch Apples

Ingredients:

5 pcs of apples; quartered, pared and cored

1/2 tsp of vanilla

1/2 c of water

1/2 Tbsp of cornstarch

1/2 - 1 Tbsp of butter

3/4 c of milk

2/3 c of brown sugar

1/8 tsp of salt

Instructions:

Combine water & sugar in saucepan, bring to a boil. Once it boils, you add apples in. Gently boil, covered 'til apples becomes tender. Take away apples gently from syrup w/ the use of skimmer.

Transfer apples in small dessert bowls.

Mix cornstarch and milk thoroughly in separate pan. Stir & cook 'til mixture boils, and pour into previously made syrup.

Boil it for few mins. Add in vanilla, butter & salt, stirring well.

Once done, pour sauce all over apples.

Fruit Salad

Ingredients:

Sweet and ripe apples; peeled and cored

Bananas; skinned and sliced

Oranges; peeled and quartered

Grapes; stalks removed

Fresh orange juice

Castor sugar (optional)

Instructions:

Remove pips and skin of oranges. Slice apples thinly. Have grapes washed and dried.

Alternately arrange and combine fruits into Pyrex bowl, in several layers. Pour freshly squeezed orange juice over salad. Additional fruits that are abundant for the season can also be added.

Add sugar and finely chopped nuts as you please.

Green Apple Pie

Ingredients:

Peeled apples; cored and sliced

1 tsp of cinnamon

1 Tbsp of flour; sifted

2 Tbsps of water

Butter

Pie paste

Ready-made pie crust

Instructions:

Sprinkle sugar, cinnamon, and flour all over apples. Add in little amount of the butter and water. Combine well.

Scoop into pie-plate lined w/ paste and cover w/ crust on top. Bake for 40 mins.

Irish Apple Pie

Ingredients:

Cored apples

Brown sugar

Cinnamon or cloves; pounded

Lemon rind; grated

Marmalade juice

Water

Puff paste

Ready-made pie crust

Instructions:

Cut cored apples into 4 or 8 pcs, depending on size. Arrange neatly on top of pie in bake dish. Season w/ spice of choice or lemon rind.

Squeeze in small amount or marmalade to add flavor. Pour in little amount of water then cover w/ paste, then bake it for 60 mins.

Mock Apple Pie

Ingredients:

Boston cracker

Cold water

Fine white sugar

Lemon orange and pulp from 1 lemon

Lemon peel; grated

Nutmeg

Instructions:

Have 1 large cracker finely crushed using w/ rollin' pin. Place in mixing bowl then add a teacupful water, a teacupful sugar, nutmeg, lemon pulp, lemon juice & half of lemon peel.

Line pie plates w/ 1/2 of puff-paste then pour mixture in. Cover w/ paste, then bake for 30 mins.

Preserved Apples

Ingredients:

Bellflower apples (ripe); pared and cored

Loaf sugar

Lemon rind

Lemon juice

Instructions:

Weigh apples: Every pound of fruit is equivalent to one pound sugar.

Place apples in stewpan filled w/ enough water to have apples covered. slowly boil them for 30 mins. Strain apples, allowing the water to mix w/ sugar in a kettle. Once sugar melts, bring to a boil adding in thinly sliced lemon rind (4 lemons for 12 apples).

Once syrup is thick and very clear, skim carefully. Add apples in. continue boiling, after 15 mins, add lemon juice. Boil for another 15 mins or 'til apples become clear & tender.

Once cooled, transfer into stone jars then tightly cover. Set for 7 days. After one week, boil again using same apple syrup.

Simple Apple Dessert

Ingredients:

4 pcs red apples (sweet); cored

water (Spring)

Cinnamon

Instructions:

Grate 2-3 cored apples. Combine apples & spring-water into mixer and pure.

Have the rest of your apples sliced into small cubes then transfer in serving bowls. Pour apple-pure all over apple cubs and dust w/ cinnamon prior to serving.

Spiced Baked Apples

Ingredients:

5 pcs apples; washed and cored

5 Tbsps of sugar

1 pc of lemon; sliced

Water

Cloves (whole)

Instructions:

Stick 2-3 cloves into every apple. Arrange them on baking dish. Put a heaping tablespoonful sugar into every whole from which you removed the core, and place 1 lemon slice on top.

Pour enough amount of water, covering baking dish's bottom. Bake them covered at four hundred degrees Fahrenheit 'til soft.

Best when served cold.

Stewed Apples

Ingredients:

12 green tart apples; cored and sliced

1 c of loaf sugar

Pinch of maze

12 whole cloves

Instructions:

Place apples in saucepan filled w/ enough amount of water to have apples covered. Cover saucepan. Stew apples 'til clear and tender.

Remove from pan and transfer into deep bowl, covered. Add1 c of sugar into sauce inside pan. Boil for 30 mins. Add a small pinch mace & all cloves, 10 mins before removing from heat.

Pour over apples immediately while hot then set aside to completely cool.

9 789334 329100

Printed at Repro India Ltd.